LEADING WOMEN

Shirley Chisholm

LUCIA RAATMA

Marshall Cavendish
Benchmark
New York

Marshall Cavendish International (Asia) Private Limited, 1 New Industrial Road, Singapore 536196 • Marshall Cavendish International (Thailand) Co Ltd. 253 Asoke, 12th Flr, Sukhumvit 21 Road, Klongtoey Nua, Wattana, Bangkok 10110, Thailand • Marshall Cavendish (Malaysia) Sdn Bhd, Times Subang, Lot 46, Subang Hi-Tech Industrial Park, Batu Tiga, 40000 Shah Alam, Selangor Darul Ehsan, Malaysia

Marshall Cavendish is a trademark of Times Publishing Limited
All websites were available and accurate when this book was sent to press.

Library of Congress Cataloging-in-Publication Data
Raatma, Lucia.
Shirley Chisholm / by Lucia Raatma.
p. cm. — (Leading women)
Summary: "Presents the biography of Shirley Chisholm against the backdrop of her political, historical, and cultural environment"—Provided by publisher. Includes bibliographical references and index.
ISBN 978-0-7614-4953-9
1. Chisholm, Shirley, 1924-2005—Juvenile literature. 2. African American legislators—Biography—Juvenile literature. 3. Women legislators—United States—Biography—Juvenile literature. 4. Legislators—United States—Biography—Juvenile literature. 5. United States. Congress. House—Biography—Juvenile literature. 6. African Americans—Biography—Juvenile literature. 7. Teachers—United States—Biography—Juvenile literature. 8. Presidential candidates—United States—Biography—Juvenile literature. I. Title.
E840.8.C48R33 2010
328.73092—dc22 [B]
2009029673

Editor: Deborah Grahame   Art Director: Anahid Hamparian
Publisher: Michelle Bisson   Series Designer: Nancy Sabato

Photo research by Connie Gardner

Cover photo by Manuel Balce Ceneta /AP Photo
The photographs in this book are used by permission and through the courtesy of: *Getty Images*: Hulton Archive, 1, 74, 6, 11, 12, 19, 22, 45, 60, 65, Popperfoto, 29, 55; Martin Mills, 31; Time and Life, 39, 50, 62, 71, 82; Diana Walker, 81; R. Diamond, 83; Scott Ferrell, 85; *AP Photo*: 4, 37, 40, 87; *Corbis*: Jonathan Blair, 9; Joseph Schwartz, 16, 24; Bettmann, 72; *Daily News Pix*: 49, 77; *Mount Holyoke*; Copyright held by Mount Holyoke College 2005. All rights reserved.

Printed in Malaysia (T)
135642

CONTENTS

Shirley Chisholm appears at an event soon after being elected to Congress in 1968. At that time, few women held professional positions.

A Strong Voice

Some people in this world are not afraid to take a stand.

They are quick to challenge situations that are unfair or unjust. They try to change the way things are instead of just complaining. One of these people was Shirley Chisholm.

When Chisholm was a young woman in Brooklyn in the 1930s and 1940s, very few African Americans held political positions. Slavery had ended in 1865, but most black Americans were not allowed to vote. Women had just earned the right to vote in 1920. It is safe to say that white men controlled all levels of American government.

Racial segregation was still the norm in the United States. Most African Americans faced poverty and held low-paying jobs. Women like Shirley Chisholm were expected to be mothers, maids, secretaries, or teachers. Few people saw them as future political leaders.

So imagine the scene when this smart, outspoken black woman, an elected member of the New York State Assembly, decided to run for the U.S. House of Representatives. Imagine what people thought when she campaigned and gave speeches. Imagine how other candidates reacted to her. And imagine the atmosphere on the night of November 5, 1968, when Shirley Chisholm became the first African-American woman to be elected to Congress. She addressed her supporters with this simple message: "As a United States Representative in Washington, I intend to represent all the people—the blacks, the whites, the men, the women, and especially the youth. There are many new ideas abroad in this country, and I intend to speak for those ideas. And my voice will be heard."

CHAPTER ONE

Early Life

THE 1920S WERE A TIME OF PROSPERITY for many people in the United States. Known as the Roaring Twenties, it was an era of music, dancing at parties, and new cars. It was a fun time, but money was short, and many people were struggling to support their families. This was the case for Charles and Ruby St. Hill of Brooklyn, New York.

The St. Hills had three daughters. The oldest was Shirley, who was born on November 30, 1924. Charles worked as a baker's assistant, and Ruby made some money as a seamstress, but they found it hard to pay the rent and provide for their girls. So they made a very difficult decision. They decided to send Shirley and her younger sisters, Odessa and Muriel, to live with Ruby's mother on the island of Barbados, where Ruby had been born and raised. They knew that Grandmother Seale would take care good care of the girls, and they hoped to save money to buy a home while the girls were away.

AT HOME IN BARBADOS

Shirley was just three years old when she and her sisters, accompanied by their mother, made the trip from Brooklyn to Barbados. The trip took nine days on a big, crowded steamship, and many of the passengers got seasick. Once they arrived in Barbados, the girls realized that their new home was a lot different from Brooklyn. Their grandmother's home was on a farm

These island children smile for the camera. When Shirley and her sisters were sent to Barbados, they grew up with children such as those pictured here.

outside a small village. She raised chickens, had a vegetable garden, and relied on an outdoor well for water.

For six months, Ruby stayed and helped her daughters get adjusted. Then she said a tearful good-bye and returned to Brooklyn. The girls were too small to understand what was happening, and Grandmother Seale made them feel at home. Soon four of their cousins—children of Ruby's older sister, Violet—joined them. The seven children were cared for by their grandmother, as well as by Aunt Myrtle and Uncle Lincoln.

When she was about four years old, Shirley started attending school in Barbados. Since the island was then part of the British Commonwealth (it gained its independence in 1966), the school had British traditions. She took classes in reading, writing, arithmetic, and history, and each day the students sang "God Save the King." Though Shirley was quite young, her school was not like today's preschool or kindergarten. The teachers were strict, and they kept a rigorous schedule. The children all wore school uniforms, as they still do in Barbados today.

After school each day, Shirley went home and joined her sisters and cousins for chores. They gathered eggs, fed the animals, and filled buckets of water from the well. They also enjoyed playing on the beautiful beaches of the Caribbean island. Since the weather was always warm, they could swim year-round. Each Sunday, the family put on their best clothes and went to church, often to three separate services. Then they shared a big meal when they got home.

Seven years later, in 1934, the St. Hills longed to reunite their family. The United States was suffering from the Great Depression, a difficult economic time when many people were out of work. But the family did not want to be apart any longer. Ruby once again traveled to Barbados. Grandmother Seale was happy to see Ruby, but she was

Students in Barbados wear uniforms to school, just as Shirley did when she was a girl.

also very sad. When Ruby and the girls left, the Grandmother Seale knew she might never see them again.

Shirley St. Hill found Brooklyn to be a huge change from Barbados. Brooklyn is one of the five boroughs, or sections, of New York City. The streets were noisy and crowded, and there were tall buildings all close together. At age ten, she found the street signs confusing, and she got lost more than once.

THE GREAT DEPRESSION

The Great Depression was the worst economic downturn in modern history. Most experts consider October 29, 1929—the day the U.S. stock market crashed—the starting point of this era. The Great Depression affected countries all over the world. The economy suffered unemployment and decreased industry. Farms failed, banks closed, and many people lost their homes. President Franklin D. Roosevelt created the New Deal during this time. This was a government-supported work program that gave people jobs to help build

Sharecroppers make their home along a highway during the Great Depression.

roads, bridges, state parks, schools, and other structures. In the United States, the Depression began to ease during World War II (1939–1945), when U.S. industries produced supplies for the military.

A family poses in front of their home in Brooklyn during the 1930s. Shirley and her family lived in a neighborhood like this one.

As the oldest daughter, Shirley knew she needed to help care for her younger siblings. In addition to Odessa and Muriel, another sister, Selma, had been born while they were away.

IN BROOKLYN

At public school in Brooklyn, Shirley benefited from the education she had received in Barbados. The teachers were impressed by how advanced she was in reading and writing. But she had studied British history in Barbados, so she knew little of U.S. history. She knew very little about the American Revolution or the Civil War. After some extra help, however, she quickly caught up to her grade level.

Shirley and her sisters were encouraged to study hard. Their father had a new job, working long hours in a burlap factory, and he wanted his children to have a good education so they could get better jobs. In Barbados, they had had chores to do around the house. But in Brooklyn, their parents told them that their job was to do well in school. The St. Hill girls were also expected to go to church each Sunday.

Besides going to school and church, the girls found time to have fun. On Saturdays, they enjoyed going to movies. In those days, movie theaters showed cartoons before a film began, and many of the films were serials. That means that the story continued from movie to movie. So people were eager to come back to theaters week after week to see what would happen next. The girls' cousins from Barbados also had moved back to Brooklyn, so all the children could play together. During the warmer months, they enjoyed spending time at the beach on Coney Island.

GROWING UP

When Shirley was about twelve years old, she and her family moved from the Brownsville section of Brooklyn to Bedford-Stuyvesant. In this neighborhood, there were more black people than there had been in Brownsville. And their new apartment had steam heat, so it was not as cold as the old one. But to make ends meet, Shirley's mother took a job as a maid. This meant that Shirley had to help take care of her younger sisters. She had her own key to their home, and it was her responsibility to walk her sisters home for lunch and after school each day. Then she looked after her sisters while her parents worked. Shirley knew that her family depended on her.

After finishing junior high school in her neighborhood, Shirley enrolled in Girls' High School. It was also in Bedford-Stuyvesant, but she had to ride a bus to get to it. She quickly made new friends, and she did well in her classes—she even earned a spot in the honor society. There were some students, however, who teased Shirley for her West Indian accent. She spoke differently from many people in Brooklyn, and sometimes they laughed at her for it. But she tried to ignore their petty remarks and spent her time reading—often as many as ten books a month.

During these years Shirley went to lots of parties, and she loved to dance. For a time, her parents worried about her. They didn't let her stay out late, and they made it clear that they expected her to make something of her life. But they appreciated her love of music, so they managed to buy a second-hand piano that Shirley learned to play.

While Shirley was in high school, the United States became involved in World War II. Lots of men joined the military, so women pitched in by running farms and working in factories to produce supplies for the war. At the same time, though, they still had to take care of their families. During this time in U.S. history, most women were not expected to work outside the home. They were wives and mothers, and sometimes teachers and nurses, but there were few female doctors, lawyers, and other professionals. But black women—like Shirley's mother, who worked as a maid—had been employed outside the home long before World War II.

The St. Hills encouraged their daughters to go to college and learn all that they could. Shirley had good grades in high school, so she was offered scholarships to colleges such as Vassar College in Poughkeepsie, New York, and Oberlin College in Ohio. The scholarships would cover tuition but not a dormitory room, meals, or books. Shirley really wanted to go away to school and test her independence, but she knew her family couldn't afford it. So Shirley decided to attend Brooklyn College, which was nearby in the Flatbush neighborhood. Tuition was free for New York City students, and Shirley could live at home. At Brooklyn College, Shirley St. Hill entered a world that would change her life forever.

CHAPTER TWO

Becoming a Teacher

PROSPECT RESTAURANT 1767
PROSPECT PLACE RESTAURANT
Coca-Cola
Coca-Cola

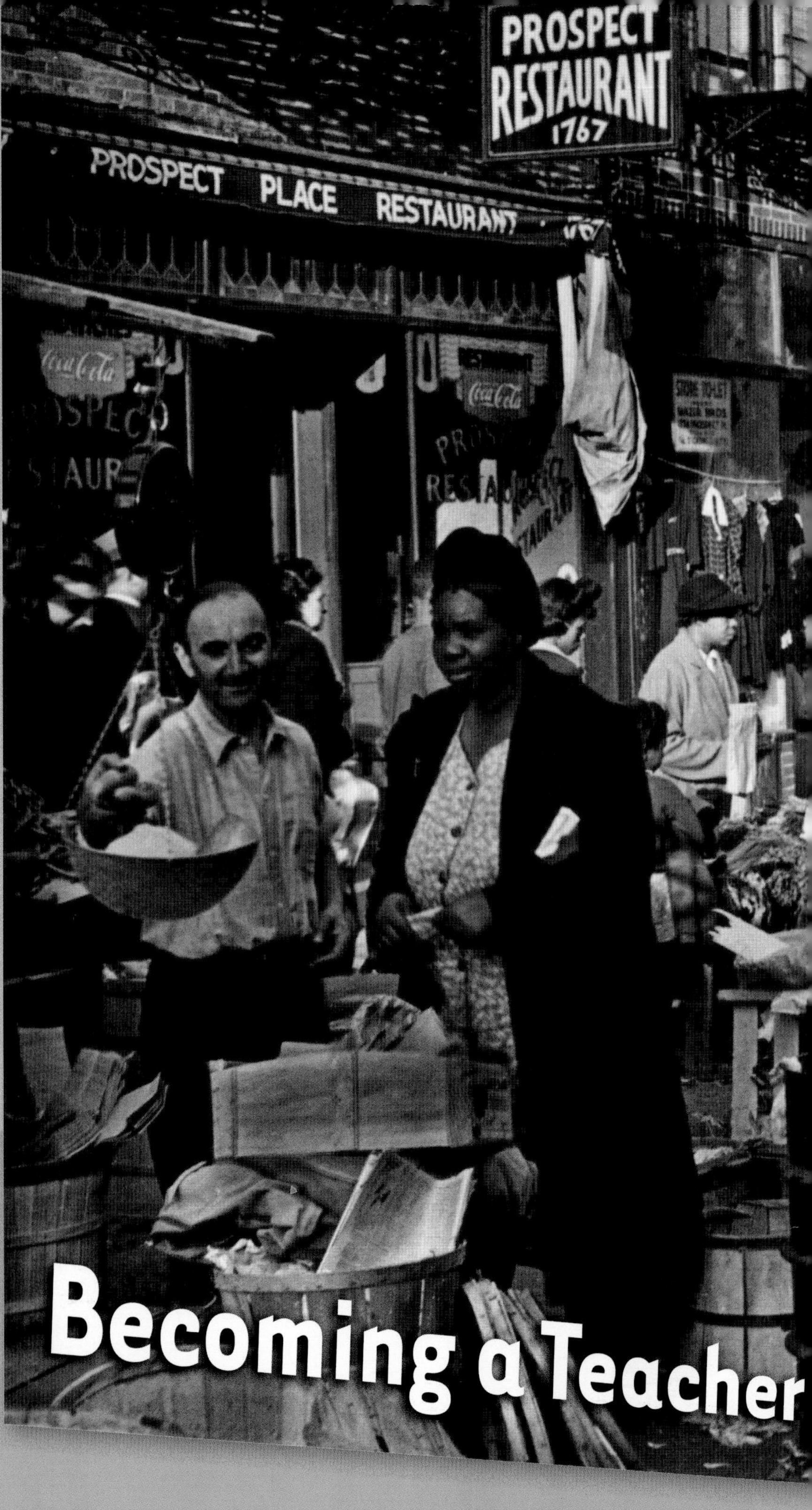

WHILE GROWING UP IN BROOKLYN, Shirley had been aware of racial differences and prejudice. She had lived in neighborhoods with both black and white people, but she knew that everyone was not treated equally. She and her family seemed to understand that people of different races remained separate.

However, Shirley was curious about how the rest of the world felt about racial differences. Although her father was not well educated, he was an enthusiastic reader, and he often spoke about politics. He was heavily influenced by the efforts of President Franklin Roosevelt and the writings of Marcus Garvey. Garvey was a Jamaican-American political leader who founded the Universal Negro Improvement Association (UNIA), the largest organization of black people in the world.

When she entered Brooklyn College, Shirley was exposed to people from all kinds of backgrounds. But there was a very small number of African-American students. They were often left out of social clubs on campus, so they sometimes formed their own organizations. One was the Harriet Tubman Society, which was named for an escaped slave who had helped other slaves flee their masters and move to the North in the 1800s. The society discussed current events and studied the ideas of Marcus Garvey, Frederick Douglass, W. E. B. Du Bois, and other prominent black figures. Douglass was an important antislavery speaker who had escaped

Shoppers and merchants conduct business at a Brooklyn street market in the 1930s.

slavery many years earlier. Du Bois was one of the founders of the National Association for the Advancement of Colored People (NAACP). He promoted racial integration and equality.

Shirley began to learn more about African history and literature. She took time to think about her own heritage. And she started to question the racial inequality that she witnessed in the world.

TESTING HER VOICE

While in college, Shirley took a variety of courses, including some in history and political science. She also joined the Political Science Society and worked on her public speaking skills. Shirley was a small, thin woman, but when she spoke to a group, she stood straight and commanded authority. She also had an incredible memory, so she often spoke without using notes. This ability would serve her well in the years to come.

One person who took an interest in Shirley was Louis Warsoff, a political science professor. After hearing Shirley participate in a debate, he asked her if she had ever considered going into politics. She answered,

 You forget two things. I'm black and I'm a woman.

Nevertheless, Shirley was interested in politics and current events. She began to attend neighborhood meetings where city council-men and other officials often spoke. She wanted to know more about local politics and how people tried to solve problems. People were

W. E. B. Du BOIS

W. E. B. Du Bois (1868–1963) was an American scholar and political activist. Born in Massachusetts, Du Bois was also a sociology professor, writer, and historian. He worked to solve the problems of racism in the United States and served as editor in chief of *The Crisis*, an NAACP publication, for twenty-five years. This journal featured the work of prominent black authors of the early 1900s. Du Bois believed that black Americans should become well educated and challenge inequality based on race.

stunned when she sometimes asked questions that other black attendees were afraid to ask.

Shirley had chosen to major in sociology. This field taught her how societies work and how people interact. She believed this background would help her be a good teacher, a career that seemed like a realistic option for her. In addition to her studies and her club activities, Shirley also found time to volunteer in her community. Through an Urban League program, she taught arts and crafts to children and helped them put on plays. These experiences further fueled her desire to teach and to make a difference in children's lives.

ST. HILL, SHIRLEY A.
707 Kingsboro Walk, Bklyn.
33, N. Y.
Major: Sociology.
Pan-American Club; Harrie
Tubman Society; Social Serv
ice Club; Ipothia.

Shirley's Brooklyn College ID card shows that she majored in sociology and was active in a number of clubs.

One of Shirley's role models was Mary McLeod Bethune. She was a teacher in the South during the early 1900s, and she believed that African-American citizens deserved access to a good education and that they should be treated as equals in the United States.

ON THE JOB

In 1946, Shirley St. Hill graduated from Brooklyn College with honors. She was eager to begin working as a teacher, but she had a hard time finding a job. There were lots of experienced teachers looking for work, too. But Shirley was persistent and landed a job as a teacher's assistant at the Mount Calvary Child Care Center in Harlem, a neighborhood in Manhattan. Eula Hodges, the director of the school, asked her before hiring her,

> **You look so much like a child yourself.
> Are you sure you can handle a classroom?**

Shirley assured Mrs. Hodges that she could. In her new job she was assigned a class of four-year-olds. She played the piano well, and she taught the children songs and dances. She also taught older students how to sew and embroider.

Shirley's teaching career was very important to her, and she wanted to learn all that she could. So in addition to going to work each day, she went to school at night. She enrolled at the Teachers College of Columbia University in the master's program for early

MARY MCLEOD BETHUNE

Mary McLeod Bethune (1875–1955) was an educator and civil rights leader. She founded a college in Daytona Beach, Florida, that later became Bethune-Cookman University. Born to former slaves in South Carolina, she worked tirelessly to improve the lives of African Americans. She served as an adviser to President Franklin Roosevelt, and she founded the National Council of Negro Women in 1935.

childhood education. She remembered how much she had loved school in Barbados, and she wanted to pass that love of learning on to another generation.

BECOMING MRS. CHISHOLM

Meanwhile, Shirley's personal life was changing. She met Conrad Chisholm, a short, husky man whose face lit up when he smiled. He asked her out on a date, and at first she hesitated. Another man had once broken her heart, and she wasn't sure if she ever wanted to marry. But Conrad was persistent, and after some time, Shirley found herself interested in this friendly and kind man from Jamaica. Conrad was a private investigator, as well as a skilled ballroom dancer. Before long she fell for him, and he won over her family as well. In 1949, Shirley and Conrad were married. They moved into their own apartment in Bedford-Stuyvesant and began their new life together.

CHAPTER THREE

The Political World

BETWEEN HER JOB AND HER STUDIES, Shirley Chisholm was a busy woman. After teaching during the day, she attended her graduate school classes in the evening and then took the subway home. As a way to make the most of her time, she often studied during the ride back to Brooklyn. Her days were long, but she didn't mind, and she still found time to attend political meetings in her community.

During this time, political clubs played a big role in local politics. These clubs would often support candidates for city and state positions. Sometimes club leaders would be elected to the state assembly in the New York capital in Albany. But even in largely African-American neighborhoods, white members ran these political clubs. Often black residents were afraid to voice their ideas or to stand up for their rights. Even at these meetings, black and white attendees sat on opposite sides of the aisle.

JOINING THE CLUB

The Seventeenth Assembly District Democratic Club, which was in the Chisholms' district, had all white leaders. Black people went to the meetings but were not official members. Chisholm decided that this needed to change, so she requested to join the club as an official member. The other club members were surprised by her request, but they agreed and assigned her to a fundraising committee.

Many apartments in the Bedford-Stuyvesant section of Brooklyn are located above stores. Conrad and Shirley Chisholm lived on a street like this one.

MAC HOLDER

Wesley McDonald "Mac" Holder (1897–1993) was a political rebel. He was born in Guyana and moved to the United States when he was in his twenties. As a young man, Holder traveled the country and fought prejudice. In Miami he was once jailed for opposing the Ku Klux Klan, a white supremacist group. He was a reporter and editor of the *Amsterdam News*, a newspaper that was geared toward the African-American community of New York City. He also worked as a researcher for a Brooklyn district attorney. Throughout his career, Holder served as a political adviser to mayors, judges, councilmen, and members of Congress. Mayor Ed Koch awarded him New York City's La Guardia Medal in 1988.

Chisholm also became friends with Wesley McDonald "Mac" Holder, whom she had met in 1946 while she was still a student. They agreed that it was time to change the ways of Brooklyn politics. One injustice they both recognized was that all forty-nine civil judges in Brooklyn were white. This seemed unfair, since Brooklyn had a large African-American population. So Holder suggested to the Seventeenth Assembly District that the group nominate Lewis S. Flagg, a black lawyer, to be a municipal court judge. The group ignored his request and nominated a white man instead. Holder and Chisholm decided to take matters into their own hands.

Chisholm and Holder formed a committee with the goal of nominating Flagg outside the club. To get his name on the ballot, they had to collect signatures on a petition. Chisholm went door-to-door throughout her neighborhood. She told people about Flagg and got many signatures. Flagg was an experienced lawyer with a good reputation, so many people were happy to lend support.

The group successfully got Flagg's name on the ballot and then set out to encourage people to vote for him. They mailed out information about Flagg and spoke to voters in person. In the end, all the extra work was worth the effort. Lewis Flagg made history in 1953 when he was elected Brooklyn's first African-American judge.

WORKING FOR CHANGE

Holder and Chisholm were proud of their success. They decided to keep their committee together and named it the Bedford-Stuyvesant Political League (BSPL). The next year, in 1954, the league nominated a number of African-American candidates for city, state, and national offices. But change did not come that easy. Their candidates were not well known, and all of them were defeated. Nevertheless, the work of the BSPL did not go unnoticed.

Around this time, the civil rights movement gained broader support in the United States. In Montgomery, Alabama, an African-American woman named Rosa Parks was arrested for not giving up her seat to a white man on a city bus. This act helped start the Montgomery Bus Boycott, which received national attention. Leaders such as Martin Luther King Jr. urged African Americans to stand up for their rights, but only in peaceful ways.

Chisholm was becoming well known throughout her neighborhood. She was active in the BSPL, and she remained a member of the Seventeenth District Assembly Democratic Club. She also attended meetings of the League of Women Voters, the NAACP, and the Stuyvesant Community Center.

THE CIVIL RIGHTS MOVEMENT

The American civil rights movement refers to the period from 1954 to 1968. It was a time when many people joined together to try to end racial discrimination. In 1954, the U.S. Supreme Court ruled in *Brown v. the Board of Education of Topeka, Kansas*, that having separate schools for whites and blacks was unconstitutional and ordered that all public schools must be integrated.

This decision met resistance in many states, and discrimination persisted. In many states, blacks still had to use separate waiting areas in doctors' offices and train stations. They even had to use separate water fountains. In addition, some black Americans were refused their voting rights through various methods. Sometimes, they had to take unfair tests before they could vote. Other times, they were just scared away from the voting offices altogether.

Little Rock Central High School in Arkansas was forced to integrate in September 1957. Here, members of the National Guard escort African-American students inside.

In the years to come, activists held protests at segregated restaurants and marched for fair voting rights for all citizens. Laws passed during these years include the Civil Rights Act of 1964, which banned racial discrimination in the workplace; the Voting Rights Act of 1965, which restored and protected voting rights; and the Civil Rights Act of 1968, which banned discrimination in housing practices.

Chisholm earned a reputation for asking hard, even embarrassing, questions. At a political club meeting, she would question issues such as why garbage wasn't picked up on schedule in her neighborhood, even though trash was properly picked up in white neighborhoods. Or she might ask why some buildings in Bedford-Stuyvesant were allowed to have code violations, while landlords of buildings in other parts of the city were forced to improve their properties. She also did not hesitate to take her complaints to City Hall. She often led protests to express that her community in Brooklyn was being treated unfairly.

In 1958, Chisholm faced a difficult issue. Many members of he BSPL thought that it was time for their president, Mac Holder, to step down and let someone else run the group. They urged Chisholm to run for president, but Holder was not ready for that. He accused her of being ungrateful to him, and their friendship fell apart. She ran for president anyway but lost. Holder kept his position and then tried to get the nomination for New York state assemblyman. He was not successful. Before long the BSPL became inactive. Although it had existed for only about six years, it had succeeded in bringing the issues of black leadership into the political discussion. The group's efforts had a lasting impact.

REACHING CHILDREN

In the meantime, Chisholm had finished her master's degree in 1951. The following year, she got a job as director of a nursery school in Brooklyn. After only a year in that position, she became director of Hamilton-Madison Child Care Center, which was located in the Lower East Side of Manhattan. Chisholm oversaw a program for some 130 children and managed a staff of 34 employees. Five years later, Chisholm was appointed educational consultant for the New York

MARTIN LUTHER KING JR.

Martin Luther King Jr. (1929–1968) was a minister and a prominent leader in the civil rights movement. Born in Atlanta, King led the Montgomery Bus Boycott in Alabama. King believed in standing up against racial discrimination, but he supported only peaceful means of protest. He helped lead the 1963 March on Washington, which focused on racial issues. At the march he delivered his now famous "I Have a Dream" speech. In 1964, King became the youngest recipient of the Nobel Peace Prize. In 1968, his life was cut short when an assassin shot him in Memphis, Tennessee.

City Division of Day Care. In this role, she oversaw the programs of ten New York City day-care centers.

Chisholm was quick to share her views about childhood education with other people in her field. She believed that learning to read and write at an early age was critical for academic success. Others disagreed with her. They believed it was too much to ask of preschool children. But Chisholm pointed out that she could read and write at age four, and that early knowledge had made her even more eager to learn. For two years, Chisholm concentrated on her career. She urged city leaders to open more day-care centers. She worked tirelessly to convince everyone that early education was important. But by 1960, Chisholm was being pulled back into politics.

BECOMING A LEADER

In 1960 Chisholm helped form the Unity Democratic Club, which challenged the dominance of the Seventeenth District Assembly Democratic Club. Unity soon merged with the Nostrand Democratic Club, a nearby club that wanted increased city services for its neighborhood. The Unity-Nostrand Democratic Club nominated Thomas R. Jones, an African-American lawyer, for the office of state assemblyman.

Chisholm used her experience from the BSPL to teach volunteers how to gather signatures on petitions and go door-to-door to win votes. Their efforts were noticed by a number of people, including former first lady Eleanor Roosevelt, who even spoke at one of their rallies. In the end, Jones got just 42 percent of the vote and lost the race. But the new political club was just getting started.

By the next election, in 1962, the Unity Democratic Club had split with Nostrand. Again the club nominated Jones for assemblyman. As winner of the election, Jones became the first African American ever to be a part of the New York State Assembly. Suddenly, the Unity Democratic Club gained importance in the Seventeenth District, and Shirley Chisholm was one of its leaders.

Two years later, in 1964, it seemed as though Jones would easily be reelected to the New York State Assembly. He was popular, and the people of his district knew he was representing them well. That year, however, there was a position open for a civil court judge. Jones was a good lawyer, and he wanted the job. But he also wanted to be sure that his district had a strong candidate for the state assembly.

RUNNING FOR STATE OFFICE

Chisholm believed that she was the candidate her district needed. For more than a decade, she had worked on other people's campaigns and had challenged political leaders on a number of issues. She decided it was her time to step into a leadership role. However, many people expressed their doubt. Could a black woman be elected to the state assembly? It had never happened before.

Even Jones was unsure whether he should pursue the judge nomination instead of the assembly nomination. Chisholm was hurt by his indecision and by the lack of support she received from some of he Unity Club's members. But in the end, Unity nominated Chisholm for the assembly, and Jones accepted the nomination for civil court judge.

When Unity announced Chisholm's nomination, some people were shocked. African-American men, in particular, felt she had no business running for office. She should take care of her husband and leave politics to men, they argued. However, Conrad Chisholm fully supported his wife. He never believed that her place was at home. In fact, in their household, Conrad did all the cooking. He knew Shirley was capable and could do a good job in the state assembly. Also, the Chisholms had discovered that they could not have children. Conrad knew that Shirley wanted to help other people's children through teaching and politics.

Early that year, officials made an important change to election districts in Brooklyn. The districts had been divided in such a way that white people still made up the majority in each district. For instance, Bedford-Stuyvesant was divided three ways, so the neighborhood was part of three separate districts. All that changed with a Supreme Court ruling in 1964, and suddenly Bedford-Stuyvesant was no longer divided. Chisholm was campaigning for a chance to represent that district. Unity ran an intense voter registration drive to be sure that her supporters would be ready to vote on election day.

To some degree, Chisholm understood why some black men did not support her. They had been fighting for a place in American society for many years, and they longed for a day when white men did not have all the power. In their minds, they needed women to support them and care for their families. Instead of worrying about the lack of support from men, however, Chisholm concentrated on serving the needs of African-American women. She knew the problems they faced each day. They wanted to have safe neighborhoods and good schools for their children.

In September 1964, Chisholm easily won the Democratic primary. Two months later, she defeated her Republican opponent by a huge margin. She had earned a seat in the New York State Assembly and was the first African-American woman to do so. The efforts of the past ten years had paid off, and other black candidates were elected to state office as well—five assemblymen and two state senators. Change had come to New York.

The following January, Chisholm traveled to Albany to take her place in the state assembly. Conrad was proud of Shirley's accomplishments, and many of her friends from Unity knew that she would work hard for Bedford-Stuyvesant. Sadly, the rest of Chisholm's family did not take part in the celebration. Her father had died from a stroke before she had been elected, and in his will he did something that tore the family apart. Although his wife and three younger daughters received the family home that he had managed to buy, he left all of his life insurance benefits to Shirley. He believed that she would need the money for her political campaigns, but her mother and sisters were bitter about his decision. Their relationship with Shirley was never the same.

Once she got settled in Albany, Chisholm quickly took on her new responsibilities. She was appointed to the assembly's education committee, which was a good fit for her professional experience. In the state assembly, bills were introduced in committees and were then presented to the full assembly for discussion. One of Chisholm's ideas in the committee led to the Search for Education, Elevation, and Knowledge (SEEK) program, which provided college scholarships for minority students. She also sponsored a bill that helped domestic workers. Remembering when her mother worked as a maid, Chisholm knew that domestic workers sometimes lost their jobs and then had no income until they could find new ones. In 1965, it became law that employers of domestic workers had to pay for unemployment insurance, so workers would receive money if they had to find new jobs.

Chisholm also sponsored bills that provided state aid to day-care centers and raised the amount of money that local school districts

In 1965, Shirley Chisholm was one of just four women in the New York state legislature. She is shown here with the other three (from left to right): Dorothy Rose of Erie County, Aileen Ryan of New York City, and Constance Cook of Ithaca.

could spend. In addition, she helped pass legislation that protected female teachers. Before, when a teacher took maternity leave, she lost her tenure. This meant that when she returned to her position, she was treated as a beginner. In 1965, a new law ensured that female teachers could keep their tenure and years of experience after maternity leave.

To be an effective representative, Chisholm had to be in touch with the people in her community. So after spending Monday through Thursday in Albany each week, she'd return to Brooklyn each weekend. On Friday evenings, she invited the people of Bedford-Stuyvesant to meet with her at Unity headquarters. She'd listen to their problems and try to find ways to improve their lives.

Chisholm should have had a two-year term, but the district lines were redrawn again, and she had to run for office in the fall of 1965. Then she had to run again in 1966. She won both elections by healthy margins. She had gained a reputation as a capable legislator who was popular with the people. Chisholm was getting ready for something bigger.

CHAPTER FOUR

ASBURY
METHODIST
CHURCH
11th + K. ST.
WASHING

WE
MARCH
FOR
JOBS
FOR ALL
NOW!

Making History

THE 1960S WERE A TUMULTUOUS TIME. Issues of race and civil rights played a role in this era of change and challenge. In 1963, President John F. Kennedy, a supporter of civil rights, was assassinated. Five years later, in June 1968, his brother Robert Kennedy, a presidential candidate, was killed. In April of the same year, Martin Luther King Jr. had also been assassinated. People wanted to take a stand, and they wanted to make the country a better place, but there was fear and uncertainty in the air.

Chisholm grieved the losses of these fine men. However, she knew that she had to move forward, to continue the work these leaders had started. Chisholm was proud to serve in the state assembly, but she set her sights on a national role. The U.S. Congress has two parts: the Senate, which has two senators from each state, and the House of Representatives, which has a number of representatives from each state, based on population. The 1964 ruling that redrew assembly districts resulted in another opportunity for Chisholm. Her new congressional district included the Bedford-Stuyvesant, Brownsville, Crown Heights, and Flatbush sections of Brooklyn. Chisholm was the first candidate to announce her intent to run for the U.S. House of Representatives from the new Twelfth Congressional District.

Martin Luther King Jr. leads the March on Washington in August 1963. He was assassinated in 1968.

Shirley Chisholm speaks with a member of her community in 1968.
She knew the benefit of meeting people face-to-face.

Chisholm faced two other candidates in the June 1968 primary: former state senator William C. Thompson and black labor leader Dolly Robinson. Some people worried that women would split their votes between Robinson and Chisholm, thus giving Thompson an easy win, but Chisholm set out to prevent that from happening.

SETTING A STRATEGY

One of Chisholm's first steps was to analyze the population of her district. She saw that the district included groups of Latino and Jewish people. And although the majority of the residents were African-American, many of them were not registered to vote. Perhaps they felt that their votes wouldn't matter or that candidates did not have their needs in mind. Whatever the case, Chisholm set a voter registration plan in motion. She also noted that a large majority of people in her district were women. So, as she had done many years before, she met with women and assured them that she knew their problems and concerns. Unity Club organizers set up small gatherings with women so Chisholm could talk with them one-on-one.

As her campaign began, Chisholm was surprised to hear from her old friend Mac Holder. In spite of their previous differences, he wanted to support her for Congress. At that time, Adam Clayton Powell Jr. of Manhattan's Harlem area was serving in Congress. He was the first African American from New York to do so. Holder knew it was important to get more African Americans in the House of Representatives, and he believed that Chisholm should be next.

Unlike her opponents, Chisholm did not have a lot of campaign funds. She had to rely on contributions from her supporters. But she was proud that she didn't take money from big groups, and that was part of her campaign slogan: VOTE CHISHOLM FOR CONGRESS—UNBOUGHT AND UNBOSSED. She took to the streets and shook voters' hands on street corners and in stores. She attended small get-togethers and spread a message of hope. She knew that the recent assassinations of King and Kennedy had shaken people. She assured them that she would fight for the voters' interests and try to make a difference in Washington.

On June 18, 1968, the Democratic primary votes were counted. Chisholm won, but by a margin of fewer than eight hundred votes. Now she had to prepare for the general election in November. She would face James Farmer, a candidate nominated by the Liberal Party and supported by the Republican Party as well.

Farmer was a strong civil rights leader who had once served as the national director of the Congress of National Equality (CORE). This organization was formed to challenge racial segregation. It played an important role in the civil rights movement. Farmer was well known throughout New York and the country. Chisholm knew she was in for a tough fight.

TAKING TO THE STREETS

Chisholm and her supporters held marches in the streets nearly every night. They visited homes and churches. They talked to people and answered their questions. During the day, Chisholm and her volunteers would drive a sound truck through neighborhoods where she was less known. She'd take the microphone and announce,

LYNDON B. JOHNSON

Lyndon B. Johnson (1908–1973), also known as LBJ, served as vice president under President John F. Kennedy. When Kennedy was assassinated in 1963, Johnson assumed the position of president. While in office, he signed the Civil Rights Acts of 1964 and 1968, and he helped create Medicare, a medical program for elderly citizens. In 1964, he ran for and was elected president, but by 1968 his popularity had declined. During his term, the Vietnam War had escalated, and more than 500,000 U.S. troops became involved. The war divided the American people and lessened their faith in LBJ. When he chose not to run for president in 1968, the Democratic Party became even more deeply divided. Johnson passed away in 1973 after suffering his third heart attack.

> **You don't know me. I'm fighting Shirley Chisholm from a neighboring district.**
> I'm running for the new congressional seat in the Twelfth District, your district. But the power structure does not want me in Washington, and this is why I am coming to you, the people, so that you can get the message directly. The organization does not want me, but the people do.

THE 1968 DEMOCRATIC NATIONAL CONVENTION

The 1968 Democratic National Convention was held from August 26 to August 29 in Chicago, Illinois. It is probably most remembered for the protests held outside the convention and the use of police force to control the crowds.

By the time the convention was held, the nation was in turmoil. Protests against the Vietnam War were raging, the civil rights movement was still simmering, and both Robert Kennedy and Martin Luther King Jr. had been assassinated. People were angry, and they looked to the Democratic leaders to make things better. Thousands of students and other protesters went to Chicago and demonstrated against the war and other injustices. Mayor Richard Daley called in the police and the National Guard to

Protesters square off with the police outside the 1968 Democratic National Convention in Chicago, Illinois.

keep order. But tensions grew, and many protesters were beaten and sprayed with tear gas. The media attention to the turmoil overshadowed the actual political process that was taking place at the convention.

Hubert Humphrey received the party's nomination, with Edmund Muskie as his running mate. In the general election that year, they were defeated by Republican Richard Nixon and his running mate Spiro Agnew.

In the meantime, Chisholm wasn't feeling well. She was under a lot of pressure, but she didn't think it was the stress of the campaign that was getting to her. At Conrad's urging, Shirley consulted a doctor and found out that she had a tumor in her pelvis. It was not cancerous, but it had to be removed. The doctor insisted on operating right away. She hated to take time away from the campaign, but she had no choice.

As soon as she could, Chisholm got back on her feet and into the campaign. The already thin woman had lost 17 pounds (7.7 kilograms), but she was tough. She made tours of her neighborhood on her campaign truck and announced over the speakers,

> **This is fighting Shirley Chisholm, and I'm up and around in spite of what people are saying!**

HEADING TOWARD ELECTION DAY

Farmer promised voters that he would be a strong voice in Congress—a man's voice. He openly appealed to the men of the district because he figured they wouldn't want a woman to represent them in Congress. But Chisholm knew that there were ten thousand more women than men in her district, and Farmer had neglected this detail. Many women did not appreciate Farmer's message that women shouldn't be in Congress, and they gave their support to Chisholm.

In August 1968, Chisholm had the honor of representing New York at the Democratic National Convention in Chicago. She was still feeling weak, but she made the trip. At the convention, Hubert Humphrey won the nomination to be the Democratic candidate for president of the United States. But he had a rough road ahead of him. President Lyndon Johnson, who became president after John Kennedy was killed in 1963, chose not to run in 1968. This left the Democratic Party in chaos. It was up to Humphrey to unite the party and to face Richard Nixon, the Republican candidate, in the national election.

In the weeks leading up to election day, Chisholm did not back down. She pointed out that Farmer really didn't know Brooklyn; he was from Manhattan and had just rented a Brooklyn apartment during the campaign. She knew everything about Brooklyn and its people. In her fiery speeches, she showed that she was not a timid schoolteacher but rather a smart, vocal leader who would fight for the residents of Brooklyn. She and Farmer had similar views on many issues, such as education and civil rights, but they were two very different people.

On November 5, 1968, history was made. The results were in, and Shirley Chisholm beat James Farmer by 34,885 votes to his 13,777. Brooklyn had just elected the first African-American woman to the U.S. Congress. Addressing her supporters at her campaign headquarters, Chisholm promised,

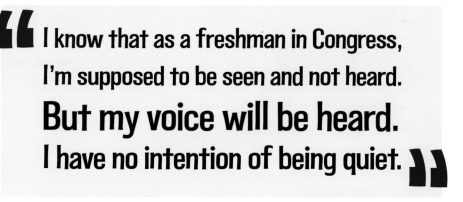

"I know that as a freshman in Congress, I'm supposed to be seen and not heard. But my voice will be heard. I have no intention of being quiet."

CHAPTER FIVE

Representative Chisholm

A FTER THE ELECTION, CHISHOLM WAS IN constant demand. She had made history, and countless reporters suddenly wanted her time. These reporters had never paid attention to her before! But Conrad knew that his wife needed some well-earned rest. They spent a few weeks in Jamaica to enjoy a vacation and to allow Shirley to fully recover from her medical issues earlier that year.

Once she was back in New York, Chisholm went to work. She needed to assemble a good staff for her Washington office. In a rare move, she assigned women to every position in her office, from assistant to high-level jobs. Some of the staffers were white, and some were black. Chisholm relied on them to keep her office running smoothly.

IN CONGRESS

In January 1969, Chisholm became an official member of the U.S. Congress. She looked forward to creating important legislation. Richard Nixon had been elected president, but the Democrats still had more members in Congress than the Republicans did. So Chisholm believed she could still help get important laws passed, and she was hopeful that Nixon would honor his promise to end the Vietnam War.

Chisholm was one of three African Americans elected to Congress that year. Another was Louis Stokes of Cleveland. He

Conrad and Shirley Chisholm share time together
at home in November 1968.

Representative Chisholm poses with members of her all-female staff at their office in Washington, D.C.

described the challenge that lay ahead of them: "It was an historic moment, which meant that we could not come into Congress and just represent our congressional districts. There was a sense of hope from minority and black Americans wherever they were. We tried to be, at that time, all things to all minorities."

Once she was in Washington, D.C., Chisholm wasted no time in learning how Congress works. She met other members of the House of Representatives, and although some were welcoming, others couldn't believe she was there. She once remembered how one male congressman constantly commented on her salary; apparently, he was amazed that a black woman could make $42,500, just as he did. Another congressman had a habit of spitting into his handkerchief each time he saw her. One day, she came up behind him quietly, pulled out a handkerchief, and spit into it loudly. "Beat you today," she said to him, and suddenly his habit stopped.

CHISHOLM'S COMMITTEE ASSIGNMENT

Committees are very important in Congress, just as they are in the New York Assembly. Chisholm hoped that she would be appointed to the Education and Labor Committee, but she was warned that many representatives wanted to be on that committee. In addition, preference was given to people who had served in Congress the longest. Chisholm thought this system was ridiculous. She thought that new members of Congress should be allowed on the important committees because they had the freshest ideas. She sent her resume to the members of Congress who made the committee selections, and she asked a member of the committee to speak to the others on her behalf.

In spite of those efforts, Chisholm was assigned to the House Agriculture Committee, specifically to a subcommittee for forestry and rural development. Chisholm was flabbergasted. What could a person from urban Brooklyn possibly contribute to this committee? In frustration she said, "The forestry subcommittee has no relevancy whatever to the needs of my constituency. Apparently all the gentlemen in Congress know about Brooklyn is that a tree grew there." This was a reference to the popular novel by Betty Smith *A Tree Grows in Brooklyn.*

Chisholm felt she had to get her assignment changed. She had been elected to Congress to help the people of Brooklyn, and people from Brooklyn needed help with urban problems. Everyone told Chisholm to be a good sport and just accept the assignment, but she would not listen. She spoke to John McCormack of Massachusetts, speaker of the House of Representatives. McCormack was sympathetic but did not get her assignment changed. Next, she decided to attend a caucus, or meeting, of representatives who had to approve the committee assignments.

It took some time before Chisholm was allowed to speak. She finally approached Wilbur Mills, the chairman of the committee. When Mills addressed her, she said that she rejected her committee assignment. The rest of the committee was astonished that she would dare press the issue. Chisholm went on to explain that she had twenty years of experience in education. She also reminded Mills that very few African Americans served in Congress at that time (9 out of 435 members), and placing them on important committees was especially important.

After the caucus, other members of Congress warned Chisholm that she might have ended her political career. But she could not just keep quiet. That was not in her nature. In the end, she was reassigned to the Veterans' Affairs Committee, which she saw as an improvement. Chisholm immediately began looking into accusations of racial discrimination in veterans' groups, and she worked to improve educational opportunities for all veterans.

SPEAKING OUT AGAINST THE WAR

As Chisholm's term began, the Vietnam War continued. President Nixon had promised to end the conflict and to bring U.S. soldiers home, but once he was in the White House, he did not fulfill that promise. Social programs began to run out of money as more government funding was used to support the war. Chisholm was very disappointed, and she worried about the young people of the United States. Many of them were being drafted into service and sent to Vietnam to fight, and there appeared to be no end in sight.

One day President Nixon made two announcements that made Chisholm realize how serious this issue was. First, he proposed that the government spend billions of dollars on a new missile system. He said that without these weapons, the United States would not be secure. Second, he said that Head Start, a preschool program for needy children, was out of funds and facing cutbacks in Washington, D.C. Right then, Chisholm saw that programs that everyday Americans needed would be sacrificed for the war.

Chisholm believed that the United States should have a strong military, but she also believed that social programs, such as those for adequate housing, food, and education, were vital for all Americans.

THE VIETNAM WAR

The Vietnam War (1959–1975) was a conflict between North Vietnam and South Vietnam. North Vietnam had communist beliefs. When the United States entered the conflict, many Americans felt that the U.S. government should not get involved. A military draft was enacted. This forced men eighteen and older to register and possibly be enlisted for service. People throughout the United States, especially college students, protested against the war and the draft.

During the war, more than 3 million U.S. soldiers served in Vietnam, and more than 58,000 lost their lives. In 1975, the United States finally pulled out of the conflict, and South Vietnam fell to North Vietnam. By that time, the United States had spent approximately $120 billion on the war (that would be about $650 billion today). This left the government with a huge debt.

U.S. soldiers take cover during a 1967 battle in South Vietnam.

In March 1969, in her very first speech to the House of Representatives, she vowed to vote against every bill that sent money to the military. She said,

 I am deeply and unquestionably opposed to the war in Vietnam.

I consider it immoral, unjust, and unnecessary. We have been pouring out the lives of our sons and wasting the spirit and the resources of our nation to support a corrupt and dictatorial government whose citizens would reject it, if it were not protected by American soldiers.

To show my displeasure with these policies, I intend to vote against every money bill that comes to the floor of Congress that provides any funds for the Department of Defense. Any bill whatsoever, until the time comes when our values and sense of duty to the citizens is turned right side up again, until our country starts to use its wealth for people and for peace, not profits and war.

People were shocked. Some believed that Chisholm was turning her back on U.S. soldiers. She replied that she was supporting the needs of the United States.

STANDING HER GROUND

In 1969, the same year Chisholm began her term in Congress, there was a heated battle in New York City. Mayor John Lindsay, a Republican, did not get support from his party to run for another term. Lindsay decided to run as a candidate from the Liberal Party instead. His opponents were John Marchi, a Republican, and Mario Procaccino, a Democrat. Everyone expected Chisholm to lend her support to Procaccino, but she just could not do it. She felt that Lindsay would be a better mayor for the people she represented. Both Conrad and Mac Holder urged her to stay out of it, but Chisholm didn't keep quiet. She made an appearance at one of the mayor's press conferences and announced her support for him. Her fellow Democrats were furious, but Lindsay won the election.

While she was in Congress, Chisholm focused on concerns she thought were specific to African Americans and women. Since there were so few African Americans in the House of Representatives, many blacks throughout the country approached her with their problems and issues. They knew she could relate to them. Women's rights activists also saw Chisholm as an ally and sought out her support.

One issue in particular was a woman's right to choose to end a pregnancy. In the late 1960s, abortion was illegal in many states. But the issue was so controversial that many legislators did not come out for or against it. Chisholm listened to both sides of the argument. Some people felt that abortion was murder, no matter how early in the pregnancy. Others felt that a woman should have the right to end a pregnancy if she was not ready to be a mother for financial, emotional, medical, or other reasons.

In the end, Chisholm agreed to try to help change the current legislation, which made most abortions illegal. She worried about desperate women who would try to end a pregnancy themselves or with the help of an inexperienced doctor. She also believed in safe family planning programs. It wasn't until 1973, with the Supreme Court decision *Roe v. Wade*, that abortion became legal throughout the country.

Another controversial issue was the idea of equal rights for women. Throughout the United States, women argued that they should be allowed the same opportunities as men and be paid the same for doing the same jobs. Chisholm addressed the House of Representatives in support of the Equal Rights Amendment. She pointed out that women made up more than half the U.S. population, but they held only 2 percent of managerial positions in the country. She further asserted,

As a black person, I am no stranger to race prejudice. But the truth is that in the political world I have been far oftener discriminated against because I am a woman than because I am black.

The Equal Rights Amendment never passed; however, women have made great strides in attaining equality in the decades since Chisholm made this speech.

ADDRESSING THE STUDENTS

Many college students were encouraged by Chisholm's views on women's rights and the Vietnam War. They hoped she was ready to make a difference. Her office began to get requests from students all over the country. They wanted her to speak at their campuses. She had to turn down a lot of these requests because she just did not have time to accommodate them all. Within her first two years in Congress, however, she had made more than a hundred such speeches.

Chisholm also welcomed students to her office, when her schedule would allow it. One day in May 1970, she sat with some students. She answered their questions and talked to them about current issues. One topic on their minds was the voting age, which Chisholm thought should be lowered to eighteen from twenty-one. (A law to do just that was passed later that year.) They also talked about the war in Vietnam, and Chisholm mentioned that few young African Americans actively protested against the war. She said,

Black people do not see this as their thing.

They see it as a middle-class problem, when it really affects all people. But black people have so many here-and-now problems—they do not see that much of the money to solve their problems is tied up in the war. It's not a philosophical thing to them. It's a white man's thing.

The same is true of Earth Day, that nationwide demonstration supporting clean air and water. They don't see what people are getting so upset about. They see white people going enthusiastically from one issue to another. From war to Earth Day, still by-passing equal rights. One eighty-five-year-old lady summed up the whole feeling in one statement: 'Polluted water, polluted air. I'm not going to get caught up in that. What we need a campaign in America about is polluted hearts. That's what's worrying black people.'

Shirley Chisholm addresses a group of war veterans on the Washington Mall in April 1971.

Throughout the United States, many people were feeling discouraged. They wanted the war and the draft to end, they still were mourning the deaths of Martin Luther King Jr. and both Kennedys, and they did not have faith in Richard Nixon. Before long, people started asking Chisholm if she would run for president in 1972. At first she brushed off the idea. She reminded her supporters that neither an African American nor a woman had been president yet—and she was both. But the questions kept coming.

All over the nation, more black politicians were gaining power. There were black mayors in Indiana and Ohio, and many African-American activists were becoming well known. More black legislators had been elected, raising the number in the House of Representatives to thirteen. These lawmakers came together to form the Black Congressional Caucus.

In the fall of 1971, a number of black leaders had a meeting in Northlake, a city near Chicago. They hoped to come up with an action plan for the 1972 election. But by the end of the meeting, the leaders had made no clear decisions. In any case, this group of mostly black men remained convinced that Shirley Chisholm would

Chisholm and other members of the Congressional Black Caucus listen to Charles Diggs speak to the press after meeting with President Richard Nixon in 1971.

be more committed to issues concerning women than to issues concerning African Americans.

In the meantime, Chisholm continued to get letters encouraging her to run for president. These requests came from women, students, Hispanics, and a wide range of everyday people. Chisholm knew she didn't have the backing of an organized group, but maybe running for the people was enough. She explained,

> **The endorsements I have so far come from those who are not regarded as leaders. . . . My backing is from just plain people, and this is enough for me. This will be my inspiration, if I do make the decision to accept the challenge.**

Launching a campaign for president was very expensive. In those days, it would cost hundreds of thousands of dollars. Chisholm and her husband did not have that kind of money, nor did she have wealthy supporters.

To become the Democratic nominee for president, Chisholm would have to perform well in the 1972 primaries and gain as many delegates as she could. Each state has a set number of delegates, usually based on population, and these delegates vote on candidates for their states. Did Chisholm have the nerve to run for the Democratic nomination? No woman had ever actively sought a major party's nomination for president. Did she have what it would take?

Chisholm made her decision official on January 25, 1972. At a press conference in Concord Baptist Church in Brooklyn, she announced,

I stand before you today as a candidate for the Democratic nomination for the Presidency of the United States. I am the candidate of the people.

Her husband, Mac Holder, and other supporters stood by her side, and reporters hung on every word. Shirley Chisholm had made history again.

In March 1972, the National Black Political Convention was held in Gary, Indiana. Chisholm was invited, but she feared she would be too much of a distraction, so she sent Thaddeus Garrett, an aide from her campaign. Many people believed she made a mistake by not attending the convention. Several thousand people were in attendance, including major names in African-American politics, such as Jesse Jackson, Coretta Scott King (widow of Martin Luther King Jr.), Richard Hatcher (mayor of Gary, Indiana), and U.S. representatives Ronald Dellums, Louis Stokes, and Charles Diggs. In the end, the convention decided not

Chisholm announces her intention to run for the Democratic nomination for president of the United States on January 25, 1972.

to endorse any of the candidates who were running for president. Chisholm was sure that this group, mostly men, was not ready for a female candidate.

Chisholm hoped to do well in some of the early primaries and to gain some attention throughout the country. But she did not have enough money to visit every primary state or to enter every primary. So she concentrated on the states where she thought she had the best chances. With that in mind, she skipped the first primary, held in New Hampshire, and set her sights on the Florida primary.

The primary in Florida was chaotic, with thirteen candidates involved. As Chisholm toured the state, enthusiastic crowds greeted her. Her message of hope and change appealed to people of many different backgrounds. But other people just did not understand why she was in the race. Even her old friend and fellow candidate, former New York City mayor John Lindsay, accused her of taking votes away from him. One day, she was not allowed to speak at a church where she was scheduled. The African-American pastor told her,

❝ We've got Hubert Humphrey. We don't need you. ❞

In addition, the lack of funds for Chisholm's campaign became a problem. Most people working for her were volunteers, and they were hard to organize. In the middle of campaigning in Florida, Chisholm's campaign manager resigned. The volunteers were left without direction, and many of Chisholm's appearances were poorly publicized—if they were publicized at all. She had hoped to earn at least 5 percent of the vote in Florida, but she ended up receiving just 4 percent. But that was enough to keep her going.

Some people questioned why Chisholm was really running for the nomination. The other candidates sometimes perceived her as a bother or a distraction. In her book *The Good Fight*, she explained it this way:

Of course my candidacy had no chance.
I had little money and no way of raising the funds it takes to run for high office. I had no big party figures supporting me. To the extent that they noticed me at all, the movers and shakers wished only that I would go away. The wild card, a random factor that might upset some detail of their plans, an intruder into the real contest among the white male candidates. Their response was ridicule—in private, not in public, because a gentleman doesn't make fun of a lady and a politician doesn't want to risk losing the black vote. **But their attitude came through clearly: treat her with respect, but of course you don't have to take her seriously.**

During the campaign, Chisholm had difficulty juggling all her responsibilities in Congress. She had finally earned a spot on the Education and Labor Committee, and she knew it was important to be present for votes and other activities. Sometimes she had to cancel campaign appearances.

Chisholm received support from the National Organization of Women (NOW), but not all of the group's members endorsed her. Some of them, including now-famous feminists Bella Abzug and Gloria Steinem, looked at the election in practical terms. They really wanted Richard Nixon out of the White House, so they felt they had to back the candidate who had the best chance to win. In most people's minds, that candidate was George McGovern.

When the Black Panthers offered Chisholm their support, she was criticized for welcoming it. The Black Panthers was a group founded to promote African-American power, and some people considered them to be radical. But Chisholm challenged Americans to consider why the group had been formed in the first place. If society had not treated black citizens so unjustly, the Black Panthers never would have existed.

As she visited states all over the country, Chisholm experienced small victories. She made a respectable showing in Massachusetts, which earned her seven delegates. And she won eight delegates in Minnesota, the home state of another candidate, Hubert Humphrey. But her Wisconsin state coordinator quit in frustration and joined the McGovern campaign.

Another opponent in the Democratic primary was George Wallace, the governor of Alabama. Best known for his full support of segregation, Wallace believed wholeheartedly that black and white students should attend different schools. On May 15, in the midst of campaigning in Maryland, Wallace was shot. He survived, but he

THE CHISHOLM TRAIL

During the campaign, one of Chisholm's staffers
wrote and a recorded a song about her candidacy.
Here are some of the lyrics:

If you're looking for a road to freedom
Take the Chisholm Trail
Of peace and equality
Take the Chisholm Trail

Proposition Coalition
Students, brothers, black, and white
She will get us out of Vietnam
She will set our women free
Reach out to the minority . . .

was paralyzed and remained in a wheelchair for the rest of his life. Chisholm disagreed with his politics, but she regretted that someone would try to kill Wallace because of his beliefs. She even visited him in the hospital to express her concern.

After the incident with Wallace, the U.S. Secret Service immediately offered Chisholm protection. They realized that Chisholm could also be a target of hate. She often received threatening letters from people who didn't think she was fit to run for president. Conrad Chisholm worried about his wife's safety, and he welcomed the Secret Service agents. Shirley may actually have been afraid, but she appeared to have no fear.

CHISHOLM '72: UNBOUGHT AND UNBOSSED

In February 2005, a documentary film titled *Chisholm '72: Unbought and Unbossed* was broadcast on public television. Directed by African-American filmmaker Shola Lynch, the movie follows Chisholm's 1972 race for the Democratic presidential nomination. In 2004, the film had been featured at the Sundance Film Festival, and in 2006, it won a Peabody Award for excellence in television programming.

The California primary was different from primaries in other states. In other states, delegates were divided up among candidates, depending on how many votes they got. But in California, the winner of the primary received all 271 of the state's delegates. Chisholm did not want to enter the California primary, but Congressman Ronald Dellums, a supporter from the Black Congressional Congress, was from California, and he encouraged her to try. The California delegate system was being challenged, so Chisholm entered after all. She ended up coming in third.

AT THE CONVENTION

As she approached the Democratic National Convention that July, Chisholm had just twenty-eight delegates. But she hoped that she might receive some from California, when the delegate issue was resolved, and perhaps some undecided delegates as well.

A supporter holds a Shirley Chisholm sign at the 1972 Democratic National Convention in Miami, Florida.

Democratic presidential nomination candidates appear on *Meet the Press* in July 1972. Shown are (top row, left to right) Senator George McGovern, Senator Hubert Humphrey, Senator Edmund Muskie, and (bottom row, left to right) Senator Henry Jackson and Representative Shirley Chisholm.

At the convention, states are called one by one to cast their votes for the candidate they choose. If a candidate does not receive enough votes in the first ballot (in this case, 1,509 votes), then a second ballot is held, and delegates can change their votes and choose whomever they like. Chisholm's strategy was to win as many delegates as possible in the first ballot in order to force a second ballot, then to meet with McGovern, the frontrunner, and offer him delegates in exchange for promises if he won the White House. She would press him to adopt certain policies on issues such as Head Start and getting out of Vietnam. Chisholm knew that a key component of politics was the willingness to bargain and make a deal.

Once Chisholm was at the convention, supporters greeted her and she enjoyed the excitement. But her plans for collecting delegates did not work out. Walter Fauntroy of the Black Caucus urged all the uncommitted delegates to vote for McGovern. And even Ronald Dellums, Chisholm's longtime supporter, decided to endorse

McGovern after being pressured to do so. Then the California delegate challenge was rejected, and McGovern got all of the California delegates. At that point Edmund Muskie withdrew from the process and released all of his delegates to vote as they wished. Chisholm was then surprised when Humphrey released his black delegates for the first ballot, so they could vote for her. Many saw this as just a last-ditch effort to stop McGovern.

On July 12, Percy Sutton, borough president of Manhattan, officially nominated Chisholm to be the Democratic candidate for the United States. Charles Evers, the mayor of Lafayette, Mississippi, seconded the nomination. The crowd cheered and waved banners, and the band played. Realizing how special this moment was, Chisholm was very moved. She approached the podium, addressed her supporters, and accepted the nomination. It was a symbolic victory, but a victory nonetheless. An African-American woman had been nominated to be the presidential candidate of a major party. It was an amazing first.

Chisholm had hoped she would have a strong showing in the first ballot, thus making a second one necessary, but it was not to be. In the end, Thaddeus Garrett convinced the Black Caucus to back Chisholm, and she received 151 delegate votes (about 5 percent). But in the first ballot, the Democratic Party chose George McGovern, who received 1,729 delegate votes (more than 57 percent). In November 1972, McGovern faced Republican incumbent Richard Nixon, who won the election by a landslide and remained in the White House.

After the convention, Chisholm returned to the House of Representatives and was reelected to her seat that fall. No doubt she was disappointed by her unsuccessful run for the presidency, but she was encouraged, too. She had helped American citizens rethink their perceptions of political candidates. Knowing that she still had work to do, Chisholm went back to Washington and to Brooklyn.

CHAPTER SIX

Chisholm's Legacy

I N THE YEARS TO COME, CHISHOLM FACED A number of challenges. There were still programs she wanted to create and laws she wanted to help pass. But many of her goals were not so easy to attain.

CONFLICT AND DISAPPOINTMENT

One challenge that Chisholm faced was financial. During the presidential campaign she had spent a lot of money, much of which was loaned to her. She found herself having to repay a huge debt. In order to do this, she accepted an increasing number of paid speaking engagements.

Then, in September 1973, Chisholm was informed that a government agency was investigating the use of funds during her campaign. Because they were volunteers, many members of her staff were inexperienced in campaigns, and some contributions had not been recorded correctly. Further, Conrad Chisholm had worked for the campaign without payment, so he didn't think to keep track of his expenses. In comparison to the budgets of other candidates, Chisholm's budget had been very small, so she believed that she was being unfairly targeted. Perhaps her outspoken criticism of the Vietnam War and other issues had made her unpopular with President Nixon and his administration. After Chisholm explained that any mistakes in her campaign were unintentional, the U.S. Department of

Representative Chisholm poses in her office
in Brooklyn in January 1974.

Justice eventually closed the investigation and found no evidence of wrongdoing.

Meanwhile, Chisholm faced some disappointments in Congress. A minimum wage bill she had worked on passed the House and the Senate, but President Nixon vetoed it. Also, she fought the president's efforts to close a government program that assisted minorities. The program was saved, but it suffered substantial cuts in funding.

In 1977, Chisholm faced personal conflicts. After nearly thirty years of marriage, she and Conrad announced their divorce. It is not completely clear what led to their split, but the stress of Shirley's political life may have played a role. Later that year, she married Arthur Hardwick Jr., a businessman from Buffalo, New York. They had met when they both had served in the New York State Assembly.

THE NEXT STEP

Like all members of the House of Representatives, Chisholm was up for reelection every two years. She continued to win these elections through 1980. Chisholm became a well-known and respected voice in Congress.

But in 1980, the atmosphere of Washington, D.C., changed. Ronald Reagan, a conservative Republican, was elected president, and a number of Democratic members of Congress were not reelected. Chisholm knew that the social programs she cared about could be in jeopardy. She also knew that President Reagan would probably not agree to fund new programs she proposed. She continued to do her job, but she was beginning to think about what she should do next.

That answer presented itself in May 1981, when Chisholm delivered the commencement address at Mount Holyoke College in South Hadley, Massachusetts. She was impressed by the school—the oldest

Shirley Chisholm and Arthur Hardwick Jr. enjoy a moment together in 1977, the year they were married.

women's college in the nation—and by its students. And she appreciated that the college president was a woman. During her visit, she met Joseph Ellis, twhe dean of faculty, and during the course of their conversation, she mentioned that she might be ready to leave Congress. He told her that if she ever decided to do that, Mount Holyoke would be honored to have her on the faculty. Chisholm pondered the opportunity and later visited the campus again.

After considering all her options, Chisholm made up her mind. She announced in February 1982 that she would not seek reelection the following fall. She assured the people of the United States that she would continue her work—fighting for women's rights and civil rights—but she would do it in a new role. Some people were angry about her decision. They felt as though Chisholm were abandoning the African-American cause. Whoever took her place in Congress would have to start all over again, with no seniority. Nevertheless, Chisholm had to do what she thought was best.

The next year, she became a professor at Mount Holyoke and started teaching classes on politics and women's issues. She once said,

 I want to make my students think. I want them to participate, to ask questions. They can disagree with me on anything, but I warn them to back up their arguments.

MOUNT HOLYOKE COLLEGE

Mount Holyoke College was founded in 1837 by chemist and educator Mary Lyon, who called it the Mount Holyoke Female Seminary. Lyon inspired her students with the advice, "Go where no one else will go, do what no one else will do." Today, Mount Holyoke College has a reputation as one of the finest schools in the United States. Its diverse student body is made up of approximately two thousand students from forty-eight states and almost seventy countries.

Professor Chisholm speaks with students at Mount Holyoke College in 1984.

The woman who had enrolled at Brooklyn College all those years ago, with the intention of becoming a teacher, had come full circle.

CHANGES AND CHOICES

Chisholm remained active in the Democratic Party. In 1984, she worked on the presidential campaign of Jesse Jackson. She also enjoyed spending time with Arthur in their home in upstate New York.

Chisholm's life changed again when Arthur passed away in 1986. Chisholm missed him and didn't like staying in their home without him, so she directed her energies elsewhere. She resigned from Mount Holyoke in 1987 and turned her attention to Jackson's second presidential campaign.

Ronald Reagan was leaving office in 1988, and the Democrats hoped to regain the White House. Jackson believed that he was the person for the job. Chisholm had broad appeal; fluent in Spanish, she helped Jackson win supporters in Hispanic areas as well as in rural white areas. Jackson fully recognized that he owed his ambitions to the efforts that Chisholm had put forth in 1972. She laid the groundwork for candidates who followed her.

Jackson ran a respectable campaign, but he did not receive the Democratic nomination for president, nor was he chosen to be the vice presidential candidate. Instead, Democratic presidential candidate Michael Dukakis chose Lloyd Bentsen as his running mate. Chisholm did not hide her disappointment.

FINAL YEARS

In the years that followed, Chisholm seldom slowed down. She served as president of the National Political Congress of Black Women (NPCBW). This group, which was formed in 1985, promotes civil rights and social

JESSE JACKSON

Jesse Jackson (1941–) is a Baptist minister and a civil rights leader who has run for the Democratic presidential nomination twice (in 1984 and 1988). Born in South Carolina, Jackson was active in the civil rights movement and worked with Martin Luther King Jr. In 1966, King assigned Jackson to work for Chicago's Operation Breadbasket, a program for African-American communities, and

the following year, he became the group's national director. Jackson founded both the Rainbow Coalition and Operation PUSH, civil rights programs that merged to form Rainbow PUSH. His oldest son, Jesse Jackson Jr. (1965–), is a member of the U.S. House of Representatives from Illinois.

Chisholm addresses the delegates at the 1988 Democratic National Convention in Atlanta, Georgia.

programs. It also encourages the involvement of African-American women in all levels of government. Today, the organization, now known as the National Congress of Black Women, has thousands of members, with chapters throughout the United States.

In 1991, Chisholm removed herself from the political scene and moved to Florida, where she intended to live quietly. Two years later, President Bill Clinton wanted to appoint her as ambassador to Jamaica, but she had to decline this honor due to ongoing health issues. In 1993, Chisholm was inducted into the National Women's Hall of Fame.

On January 1, 2005, the remarkable life of Shirley Chisholm came to an end. She suffered several strokes and passed away at her home in Ormond Beach, Florida. Seven days later, hundreds of people crowded the First AME Church and celebrated the contribution Chisholm made to this world. The minister explained that she made a difference because

 she showed up, she stood up and she spoke up.

Chisholm was buried in Forest Lawn Cemetery in Buffalo, New York.

Chisholm appears at the 2001 Trumpet Awards ceremony. The Trumpet Awards Foundation honors the accomplishments of African-American men and women.

LEAVING HER MARK

In her biography *The Good Fight*, Chisholm looked back to her 1972 campaign. She wrote,

 I ran because someone had to do it first.

In this country everybody is supposed to be able to run for President, but that's never really been true. I ran *because* most people think the country is not ready for a black candidate, not ready for a woman candidate. Someday. . . .

In 2008, thirty-six years after Chisholm ran her groundbreaking campaign, the U.S. presidential race was again historic. Senator Hillary Rodham Clinton, a female senator from New York, and

A painting of Shirley Chisholm is unveiled by the Congressional Black Caucus at the Capitol complex in March 2009. Present are (left to right) Representative Barbara Lee, House Speaker Nancy Pelosi, Representative Donna Edwards, and Representative Maxine Waters.

Barack Obama, an African-American senator from Illinois, were the leading contenders for the Democratic presidential nomination. In the end, Obama won the nomination, and in November of that year, voters chose him over Republican John McCain to lead the nation. Some people thought that a black person would never be elected president of the United States. But Shirley Chisholm always knew that it was possible. And her efforts paved the way for more people to try.

Chisholm once said,

 I do not want to be remembered as the first black woman to be elected to the United States Congress, even though I am. I do not want to be remembered as the first woman who happened to be black to make a serious bid for the presidency. **I'd like to be known as a catalyst for change.**

Chisholm and her campaign workers flash victory signs after her election to Congress in 1968.

TIMELINE

1924 — Shirley St. Hill is born on November 30 in Brooklyn, New York.

1927 — Moves to her grandmother's home in Barbados with her two younger sisters.

1934 — Returns to Brooklyn.

1946 — Graduates from Brooklyn College with a BA in sociology.

1949 — Marries Conrad Chisholm.

1951 — Earns her MA in early childhood education from Columbia University's Teachers College.

1964 — Is elected to the New York State Assembly (serves until 1968).

1968 — Is elected to the U.S. House of Representatives (serves until 1982).

1972	Runs for the Democratic presidential nomination.
1977	Divorces Conrad Chisholm; marries Arthur Hardwick Jr.
1983	Begins teaching at Mount Holyoke College (resigns in 1987).
1985	Helps organize the National Political Congress of Black Women and serves as its president.
1988	Campaigns for Jesse Jackson.
1991	Retires to Florida.
1993	Turns down an offer to be ambassador to Jamaica; is inducted into the National Women's Hall of Fame.
2005	Dies on January 1 in Ormond Beach, Florida.

SOURCE NOTES

Boxed quotes unless otherwise noted

INTRODUCTION

p. 5, par. 4, Brownmiller, Susan. *Shirley Chisholm* (New York: Pocket Books, 1970), p. 89-90.

CHAPTER 2

p. 18, Scheader, Catherine. *Shirley Chisholm: Teacher and Congresswoman* (Hillside, NJ: Enslow Publishers, 1990), p. 24.

p. 21, Hicks, Nancy. *The Honorable Shirley Chisholm: Congresswoman from Brooklyn* (New York: Lion Books, 1971), p. 36.

CHAPTER 4

p. 43, Hicks, *The Honorable Shirley Chisholm*, p. 68.

p. 46, Scheader, *Shirley Chisholm*, p. 75.

p. 47, Ibid, page 78.

CHAPTER 5

p. 51, par. 2, Hicks, *The Honorable Shirley Chisholm*, p. 81.

p. 52, par. 1, Ibid, p. 80.

p. 56, Ibid, p. 94.

p. 58, Chisholm, Shirley. "Equal Rights for Women" speech, U.S. House of Representatives, May 21, 1969. http://gos.sbc.edu/c/chisholm.html accessed on September 10, 2009.

p. 59, Hicks, *The Honorable Shirley Chisholm*, pp. 102-103.

p. 63, Scheader, *Shirley Chisholm*, p. 98.

p. 64, Ibid, page 100.

p. 66, Chisholm, Shirley. *The Good Fight* (New York: Harper & Row, 1973), p. 77.

p. 67, Ibid, p. 3.

CHAPTER 6

p. 78, Scheader, *Shirley Chisholm*, p. 118.

p. 82, Moore, Idella. "Looking for Shirley Chisholm," Women's eNews, January 18, 2005. www.womensenews.org/

p. 84, Chisholm, *The Good Fight*, p. 3.

p. 86, Scheader, *Shirley Chisholm*, p. 124.

FURTHER INFORMATION

BOOKS

Caputo, Philip. *10,000 Days of Thunder: A History of the Vietnam War*. New York: Simon & Schuster, 2005.

Kallen, Stuart A. *Women of the Civil Rights Movement*. San Diego: Lucent Books, 2005.

McGowen, Tom. *The 1968 Democratic Convention*. Danbury, CT: Children's Press, 2003.

WEBSITES

Black Americans in Congress: Shirley Chisholm

http://baic.house.gov/member-profiles/profile.html?intID=24

PBS: Chisholm '72: Unbought and Unbossed

For information about this PBS documentary

www.pbs.org/pov/pov2005/chisholm/

BIBLIOGRAPHY

Brownmiller, Susan. *Shirley Chisholm*. New York: Pocket Books, 1970.

Chisholm '72: *Unbought and Unbossed*. Twentieth Century Fox Home Entertainment, 2004.

Chisholm, Shirley, "Equal Rights for Women," Address to the United States House of Representatives, May 21, 1969. http://gos.sbc.edu/c/chisholm.html

Chisholm, Shirley. *The Good Fight*. New York: Harper & Row, 1973.

Hicks, Nancy. *The Honorable Shirley Chisholm: Congresswoman from Brooklyn*. New York: Lion Books, 1971.

Moore, Idella. "Looking for Shirley Chisholm," Women's eNews, January 18, 2005. www.womensenews.org/article.cfm/dyn/aid/2151/context/archive.

Reed, Brian. "Chisholm Forged a Place for Black Congresswomen," NPR.com, November 7, 2008. www.npr.org/templates/story/story.php?storyid=96516491.

Scheader, Catherine. *Shirley Chisholm: Teacher and Congresswoman*. Hillside, NJ: Enslow Publishers, 1990.

"Shirley Chisholm, 'Unbossed' Pioneer in Congress, Is Dead at 80," New York Times, January 3, 2005. www.nytimes.com/2005/01/03/obituaries/03chisholm.html.

INDEX

abortion rights, 57–58
African Americans
    gender relations and, 33–34
    politics and, 5, 57, 61, 63, 64, 66
    in U.S. House of Representatives, 49,
        51
    Vietnam War and, 59

Barbados, **6**, 7–8, **9**
Bedford-Stuyvesant Political League,
    27, 30
Bethune, Mary McLeod, 21, 22, **22**
Black Congressional Caucus, 61, **62–63**
Black Panthers, the, 68
Brooklyn, NY, 7, 9, **12**, 13–15
Brooklyn College, 15, 17–18, 20–21
*Brown v. the Board of Education of
    Topeka, Kansas* (1954), 28

campaign funds, 41–42, 63, 66–67,
    75–76
caucuses, U.S. House of Representatives
    and, 52–53
childhood, of Chisholm, Shirley, 7–9,
    13–15
Chisholm, Conrad, 23, 33–34, **48**, 69,
    76
Chisholm, Shirley, personal life of, 7–9,
    13–15, 23, 76, 80, 82
Chisholm '72: Unbought and Unbossed
    (film), 70
Chisholm Trail, The (song), 69
Civil Rights Acts (1964 and 1968), 29,
    43
civil rights movement, 27, 28–29, 31,
    81
Clinton, Hillary Rodham, 84
committee assignments, 51–53, 68

day care, 30, 32, 35, 37
Dellums, Ronald, 70, 72–73
Democratic National Convention (1968),
    44–45, **44–45**, 46
Democratic National Convention (1972),
    70, **71**, 72–73

Democratic National Convention (1988),
    82
divorce, 76
domestic workers, unemployment
    insurance and, 35
Douglass, Frederick, 17–18
Du Bois, W. E. B., 17, 18, 19, **19**

education
    college, 15, 17–18, 20–21
    elementary and high school, 8, 13, 14
    master's degree, 21, 23
    state funding for, 35, 37
    views on, 30, 32
Education and Labor Committee, 51, 68
elections
    1972 presidential campaign and, 61,
        63–64, 66–70, 72–73, 84
    2008 presidential campaign and, 84,
        86
    Jesse Jackson and, 80, 81
    of judges, 26–27, 33
    for state assembly, New York, 32–33,
        33–34, 37
    for U.S. House of Representatives, 5,
        41–43, 42–43, 46–47
employment
    Ruby St. Hill and, 14
    state legislation and, 35, 37
    teaching career, 20, 21, 23, 78, 80
    women and, 15
environmental movement, 59
Equal Rights Amendment (ERA), 58

family life, 7–8, 23, 35, 76
Farmer, James, 42, 46, 47
Flagg, Lewis S., 26–27
forestry subcommittee, 52

Garvey, Marcus, 17
Great Depression, the, 10–11

Hardwick, Arthur, Jr., 76, **77**, 80
Harriet Tubman Society, 17–18
health problems, 43, 46

ABOUT THE AUTHOR

LUCIA RAATMA is the author of dozens of books for young readers. She enjoys writing about historic events and famous people, as well as safety, environmental issues, and character education. She lives in the Tampa Bay area with her husband and their two children.